BEYOND LIMITATIONS

Acrylic paint on fabric
Detail of a painting used on a vestment.
Andre, Temple School, New Britain, Connecticut.
Age 21. Down's syndrome.
Teacher: Don Newcomb
Photographer: Maureen Kilbourne

Beyond Limitations

THE CREATIVE ART OF THE MENTALLY RETARDED

BERNI GORSKI

Foreword by

SEYMOUR B. SARASON, Ph.D.
Professor, Department of Psychology
Yale University
New Haven, Connecticut

Introduction by

BARBARA BARD, Ph.D.
Professor, Department of Human Services
and Special Education
Central Connecticut State College
New Britain, Connecticut

CHARLES C THOMAS • PUBLISHER
Springfield • Illinois • U.S.A.

Published and Distributed Throughout the World by

CHARLES C THOMAS • PUBLISHER

Bannerstone House

301-327 East Lawrence Avenue, Springfield, Illinois, U.S.A.

© *1979, by* CHARLES C THOMAS • PUBLISHER

ISBN 0-398-03897-X

Library of Congress Catalog Card Number: 78-26642

*With THOMAS BOOKS careful attention is given to all details of
manufacturing and design. It is the Publisher's desire to present books that are
satisfactory as to their physical qualities and artistic possibilities and
appropriate for their particular use. THOMAS BOOKS will be true to those
laws of quality that assure a good name and good will.*

Printed in the United States of America

R-1

Library of Congress Cataloging in Publication Data

Main entry under title:

Gorski, Berni

   Beyond limitations.

    1. Artists, Mentally handicapped. 2. Art and mental
illness. 3. Creation (Literary, artistic, etc.)

I. Gorski, Berni.

N8356.M4B49	709'.2'2	78-26642

ISBN 0-398-03897-X

To Steven
who opened our eyes
and changed our lives

FOREWORD

ALTHOUGH many changes have occurred in people's attitudes toward mentally retarded individuals, it is fair to say that the change has been largely in the direction of a more sympathetic and accepting attitude. There is now a recognition that mentally retarded individuals have rights as citizens that for too long were ignored by our society. We also hear much today about the capabilities of many mentally retarded individuals for making a productive community adjustment. However, in all of these changes one finds little or no recognition of the fact that the spark of creativity exists in many of these individuals. When one peruses the hundreds of educational curricula that have been developed in special education, one sees how strongly entrenched is the attitude that mentally retarded individuals do not have a truly creative spark. Berni Gorski's book should be a welcome antidote to these attitudes. What she has done poses two very significant questions: What does this tell us about the creative process? What does it tell us about our conceptions of mental retardation? With very few exceptions the prevailing cultural attitude is that artistic activity is a special gift of very special people, leading to the belief that only in museums and exhibits can one find works of art. Artistic activity is an attribute of all human beings but whether it is manifested depends in large measure on cultural factors. This holds as much for mentally retarded individuals as for any other group. I personally am grateful to Berni Gorski for reminding us again that under appropriate conditions this attribute can flourish.

Seymour B. Sarason, Ph.D.

PREFACE

ARE the mentally retarded capable of creative expression in the visual arts? This book, which answers *yes* to the question, was conceived as a method of disseminating information on this relatively little known subject. It hopes to encourage administrators, teachers, and parents to involve the retarded in creative activities. As a unique and compelling art collection it seeks to inspire those in charge of developing programs to explore new ways of reaching these handicapped, especially through the visual arts.

The Education Of All Handicapped Children Act, Public Law 94-142, was passed in November 1975. As schools and communities prepare to deal with the handicapped on a more integrated basis, there will be more public awareness of the retarded. Administrators, teachers, and even parents of the handicapped are not always aware of their creative potential. This book seeks to change that lack of awareness. It also seeks to encourage those working with and for the retarded to design and support programs involving them in creative experiences.

We hope that this collection will broaden the outlook of all who see it. One cannot help but be impressed and delighted by these fresh expressions of individual spirit. The expressive content of the art is a challenge that obliges us to reflect on the nature of those who created it. It is a challenge to rethink our often sterotyped and uninformed ideas about those who are developmentally disabled.

All those who enjoy art, who recognize and cherish the creative spirit, will respond to these examples from the world of the retarded. Their art enriches the lives of all by presenting another facet of our humanity to us. It allows us to really *see* again. It awakens forgotten levels of awareness and permits us to experience freshly the mystery and joy of life's simplest offerings.

B.G.

INTRODUCTION

T HE art in this book, like all art, needs neither explanation nor introduction. It speaks for itself. The labels which society has attached to the artists, however, should be explored. As the reader goes through this book, he will be presented with an array of terminology, all of it in current use, to describe and define this group of creative people. Whether or not the product jibes with the description of delay or deficiency will be for the reader to determine.

Mental Retardation: Each method of classifying the mentally retarded (IQ testing, measures of adaptive behavior, degree of impairment, form, cause, etc.) has its advocates and detractors. The most widely used definition of Mental Retardation is that of the American Association on Mental Deficiency: "Mental Retardation refers to significantly subaverage general intellectual functioning existing concurrently with deficits in adaptive behavior, and manifested during the developmental period."*

Sub Categories of Mental Retardation: Mild, moderate, and severe, when applied to mental retardation, are generally defined in terms of IQ range with adaptive behavior not included. Both AAMD studies - Heber † and Grossman (1973), – define the IQ ranges in the same way:

Mild	IQ:	70 – 55
Moderate	IQ:	55 – 40
Severe	IQ:	40 – 25
Profound	IQ:	25 – and below

* Grossman, H. J. (Ed.): *Manual on Terminology and Classification in Mental Retardation.* Washington, D.C., AAMA, 1973.

† Heber, R. F.: *A Manual on Terminology and Classification in Mental Retardation* (Rev. Ed.). American Journal of Mental Deficiency Monograph, 1959.

Down's Syndrome (formerly called "Mongolism"): A chromosomal abnormality which can generally be diagnosed at birth. Mental retardation is one of the characteristics of this syndrome. The IQ range is generally thought to be between 20 and 60. In addition to characteristically flat facial features, epicanthic folds of the eyelids, an upward slant to the eyes, and lanugoid (baby fine) hair, even in adulthood, are among the other distinguishing physical characteristics of this population.

Echolalia: A language behavior of certain retarded children where they repeat all or part of a sentence they have been told, rather than initiate an answer.

Autism: A psychiatric disorder first described by Dr. Leo Kanner, where the primary presenting symptoms in children are extremely poor or nonexistent relationships to other people; withdrawal from reality; and little or no overt language development or construction of a private language. Some controversy exists as to whether or not autistic children can be considered mentally retarded. Functionally, in their abilities to live independently, many autistic children appear to be no better able to care for their needs or make their wants known than moderate-severely retarded children.

Barbara Bard, Ph.D.

ACKNOWLEDGMENTS

THIS book would not have been possible without the cooperation and encouragement of many people. Don Newcomb, Henry Gorski, Russell Huff, and William Cavallaro were more than generous with their time and professional help. I am also indebted to Seymour Sarason, Barbara Bard, and Marguerite Lupap for their special contribution to the text.

I am happy to express my appreciation and gratitude to the following administrators, teachers, parents, and friends: Arnold Fassler, Connie Butler, Fred Schroeter, Adelle F. Headley, Joseph F. Mateju, Ann D. Clark, Henry Perea, Howard J. Chinn, Larry W. Talkington, Gentry Mohr Brazeau, G. Michael Cicatello, Edward J. Klezek, R. Allen Williams, Ann Hughes, Jo Lightfoot, David Blatchley, Christine Drozd, Bette Peterson, Eleanore Lyon, Michael Belmont, Jay Virbutis, Frank Limauro, Michael R. Dillon, Marilyn Aligata, Maureen Kilbourne, Grace Sullivan, Natalie Perry, Gilberte Lavertue, Dominic Petro, Fred Kuhne, William Doolittle, Patricia Cawley, Joan Courcey, Rose Kukhala, Justine Gonyea, Edward Benjamin, National Committee, Arts for the Handicapped, M.D., V.R., S.M.P., and D.O.

A very special acknowledgement is due the many artists whose work is included in this collection.

Berni Gorski

CONTENTS

xv

BEYOND LIMITATIONS

Chapter I ————————————

ABOUT THE ARTISTS AND THE ART

THE artists whose work is shown here are innocent of art theory, but the need to create and give form to ideas and moods is as necessary for them as it is for the rest of us.

Much has been written and spoken about the important contribution creative activities make to the growth of personality and self-confidence. Many authorities agree that we gain in self-respect and grow in independence when we are encouraged to work creatively. Purely imitative work, copying, tracing, and the like, contribute little to the growth of the individual. It is even more important that the retarded be given the opportunity to develop themselves and be encouraged to grow in a climate where creativity is allowed to flourish, despite what may seem to be limited results in terms of a finished product.

Some of the art in this collection of original work was done by those in state training schools, some by pupils in special classes in public or private schools, and some by those living at home.

The art falls into several broad categories based upon medium and type. Media include poster paint, water color, acrylic paint, and oil paint done on paper, cardboard, canvas, and canvas board; felt-tipped pen, crayon, chalk, cut paper, wood, clay, mosaic stone, papier mâché, cloth, and yarn.

One of the artists is very ingenious in finding materials on which to paint. He has used the cloth backing of vinyl upholstery fabric and has also cleverly salvaged empty bags in which rice was delivered to the training school where he lives. Another will only do his crayon drawings on cloth. When nothing else is available he uses pillow cases or peices of old torn sheets.

The themes are varied. We see figures of all kinds from portraits to imaginary images. They may be shown alone, in a familiar setting such as a schoolroom or a back yard, or in a fanciful setting alive with original use of color, form, and space. There are landscapes and still life and marvelously designed animals. Stories they have heard, trips they have taken, and special holiday activities often serve as points of departure for their art. Then again, the material itself or the mood of the moment may determine the form of expression. The work may not necessarily be representational at all.

Sam, one of the most prolific artists, showed his work to us in preparation for selection for this book. When we asked him the title of a certain painting for purposes of documentation, he replied, "I was thinking of mountains."

The Collection Begins

Several years ago, on a visit to the Southbury Training School, we noticed a display of wooden objects on a table in front of one of the cottages. A young man, one of the residents of the school, had made the objects himself, and now, on a visiting Sunday, he was exhibiting them.

The birdhouses and tie racks shown were of the run-of-the-mill kind, totally undistinguished in design but several other pieces were original in concept and worth looking at more closely. One was the figure of a man flexing his biceps. Although the wood was crudely put together, the figure had a compelling charm. There was a jaunty air of confidence in the serious expression, the bumps for muscles, and the spread-legged stance. A curved moustache added an exotic touch, as did the mysterious red dots all over the body. The figure was mounted on two simple wooden blocks which allowed the piece to stand firmly. (Figure 1.)

Another piece, more sombre in tone, was of a simple male figure painted black with blue dots for the jacket buttons. There was a slit to define the legs, but the arms were attached so they could be moved back and forth. There was an air of solidity and quiet containment about the piece, enhanced by the great economy of means used to define the forms. (Figure 2.)

A vivid pattern painted on an animal form attracted our attention. What a clever way to show alligator hide! The essential characteristics were there, emphasized by the simple shapes used to create the long, low, painted creature. (Figure 3.)

These three pieces which have become part of our art collection provided the inspiration for beginning a search to find other art done by the retarded. We believe that there is a vast quantity of genuinely creative art waiting to be discovered. The art shown here represents merely the tip of the iceberg.

Chapter II_____

THE ART COLLECTION

"ART does not come and lie in beds we make for it. It slips away as soon as its name is uttered: it likes to preserve its incognito. Its best moments are when it forgets its very name." (Jean Dubuffet)*

The photographs of the art are accompanied by descriptive identification with the specific developmental disability of the artist noted. These identifications were provided by the various schools and institutions who participated in the project. Their inclusion has been done from a positive point of view, to show that labels are not necessarily limiting. The age given is that of the artist at the time he or she did the particular work of art. In some cases the name has been changed.

With what direct, unselfconscious, and often astonishing power these artists have worked beyond the limitations of the labels they have been given!

* From *Art Brut* by Michael Thevoz © 1976 Albert Skira, Geneva. Published in the United States by Rizzoli International Publications, New York.

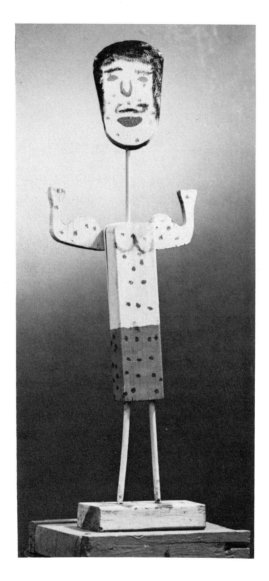

Figure 1: Wooden sculpture, painted; 27" × 9½"
Sam, Southbury Training School, Connecticut.
Age 43. Mildly retarded, epileptic.
Sam has been in various institutions almost all of his life. This and the other wooden figures were made entirely on his own.
Photographer: Henry Gorski

Figure 2: Wooden sculpture, painted; 12½" × 2½", base 6" × 7"
Sam, Southbury Training School, Connecticut
Age 43. Mildly retarded, epileptic.
Photographer: Mack McCormack

Figure 3: Wooden sculpture, painted; 18" × 4½"
Sam. Southbury Training School, Connecticut
Age 43. Mildly retarded, elileptic.
Photographer: Henry Gorski

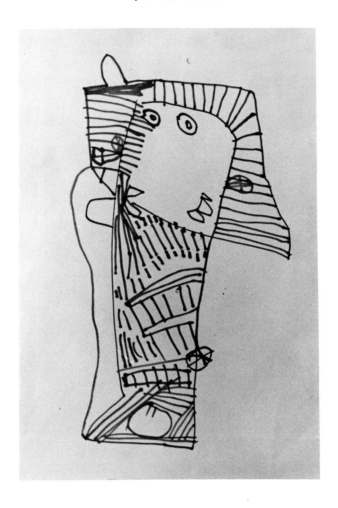

Figure 4: Green felt-tipped pen; 12" × 18"
Title: Melody
Scott, Enid State School, Oklahoma
Age 12. Mildly retarded.
Teacher: S.M.P.
"This is a drawing of another instructor in Arts and Crafts. We were told what it was only after Scott completed it."
Photographer: J.T. & S.P.

Figure 5: Water colors and crayons; 12" × 21"
Title: My Friend
Joyce, Ebensburg Center, Pennsylvania
Age 25. Mildly retarded.
Teacher: Edward J. Klezek
Photographer: Brian Smith

Figure 6: Felt-tipped pens; 20" × 30"
Title: Plainville U.S.A. 1
Andre, Temple School, New Britain, Connecticut
Age 21. Down's syndrome.
Teacher: Don Newcomb
Several years ago when Andre's parents moved from a large house in town to a smaller house in the suburbs he did these paintings of his new surroundings.
Photographer: Henry Gorski

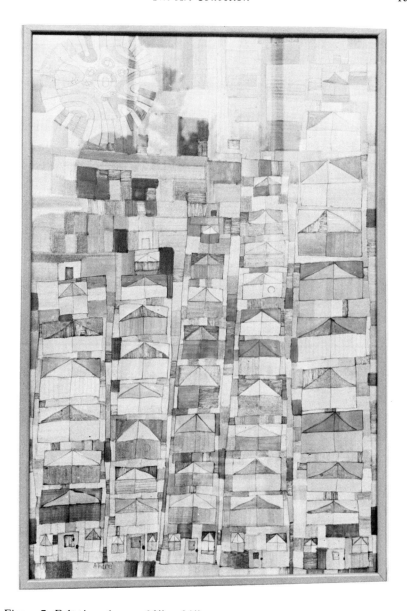

Figure 7: Felt-tipped pens; 20" × 30"
Title: Plainville U.S.A. 2
Andre, Temple School, New Britain, Connecticut
Age 21. Down's syndrome.
Teacher: Don Newcomb
Photographer: Henry Gorski

Maureen Kilbourne who did a photographic study of Andre, his art, and his environment has this to say of his work:

Andre is a young artist who communicates with simplicity and sensitivity through his intuitive use of color and form. His sureness of vision, explicit shapes, and vivid colors have given his work a uniqueness that elicits interest, curiosity, and response.

Birds, suns, figures facing the viewer directly, are predominant features found in Andre's work. Staring, unmatched eyes demand attention and often provoke intense feeling. The suns are awkward circles surrounded by linear rays. Seen from the side-view, Andre's birds seem to plunge toward another figure or into the suns. The predominant features are seen repeatedly in the artist's work and serve well in his relaying of Old and New Testament themes.

Andre deals with many geometric shapes that form symmetrical and precisely balanced patterns. Juxtaposed carefully according to size and color, these patterns cause movement and increase the vividness of the visual experience.

. . . . Andre is an artist — not a mentally retarded artist. His work stands on its own, a testimony to the fact that all men must be given the openness in which to discover who they are, why they are, and what they may become.

Figure 8: Felt-tipped pens; 16" × 20"
Andre, Temple School, New Britain, Connecticut
Age 21. Down's syndrome.
Teacher: Don Newcomb
Photographer: Paul Morton

Figure 9: Felt-tipped pens and pasted cut paper; 16" × 20"
Title: Joseph's Coat of Many Colors
Andre, Temple School, New Britain, Connecticut
Age 21. Down's syndrome.
Teacher: Don Newcomb
Photographer: Paul Morton

Figures 10 and 11: Ceramic
John T., Syracuse Developmental Center, New York.
Age 24. Severely retarded.
Teacher. Christine Drozd
Photographer: David Blatchley

Figure 12: Mixed media on canvas board; 24" x 30"
Title: Stamford Railroad Station
Sam, Southbury Training School, Connecticut
Age 39. Mildly retarded.
Photographer: Henry Gorski

Figure 13: Mixed media on back of vinyl upholstery covering; 24" × 24"
Title: Old House in the Country
Sam, Southbury Training School, Connecticut
Age 39. Mildly retarded.
Photographer: Henry Gorski

Sam and his painting are a familiar sight on the grounds of the Training School. He can often be found drawing or painting at a table in the picnic grove near the small lake, which is a scenic spot in the area. This is where we first found him thoughtfully smoking his pipe and gazing toward the low wooded hills which lie beyond the lake. That day he was working on a cityscape.

He is very serious about his art and speaks with enthusiasm about his ideas for paintings. His natural talent for composition is evident in all that he does and his talent for improvisation is revealed in his mixing of media and his resourceful use of materials to paint on.

Some of his paintings are hanging in the cottages, some in the supply store where he works, and others are stacked in the basement of his cottage. From time to time he participates in exhibits and has sold things in this way. Occasionally he even accepts a commission for a painting.

Sam reveals the assured confidence of a professional in the way he works. He knows what he wants to do and does not hesitate to do it.

Figure 14: Mixed media on rice bag fabric; 20" × 20"
Title: I Was Thinking of Mountains
Sam, Southbury Training School, Connecticut
Age 39. Mildly retarded.
A writer seeing this painting was moved to comment, "I Was Thinking of Mountains but not great imprisoning, pondering shapes blocking the horizon. Here there is a way through. The horizons are distant and inviting."
Photographer: Henry Gorski

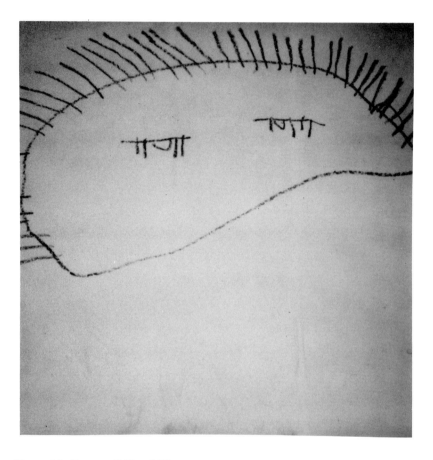

Figure 15: Crayon; 24" × 20"
Evelyn, Alaska
Age 26. Moderately retarded, deaf.
Her teacher Fred Schroeter says that although Evelyn has been institution-
alized since the age of five, the images she draws are in many ways like the
ancient ancestral folk art of her Eskimo people. She produces many variations
of this facial theme.
Photographer: Fred Schroeter

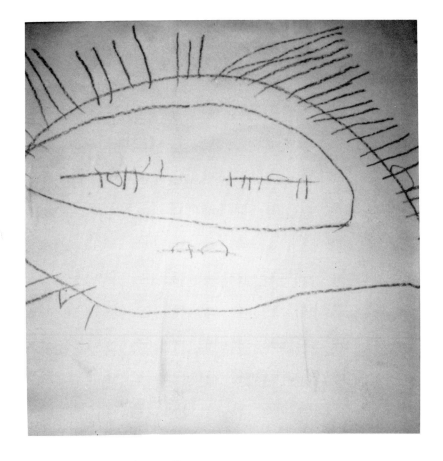

Figure 16: Crayon; 24" × 20"
Evelyn, Alaska
Age 26. Moderately retarded, deaf.
Teacher: Fred Schroeter
Photographer: Fred Schroeter

Figure 17: Felt-tipped pens; 18" x 24"
Title: San Francisco
Joan, Sonoma State Hospital, California
Age 26. Retarded, schizophrenic, brain damaged.
Teacher: Connie Butler
Joan had gone to visit San Francisco and did this picture on her return. Her teacher commented on Joan's amazing visual memory. Everything she does unfolds from top to bottom very precisely. She didn't like to draw when watched, and detested art classes or any suggestions."
Photographer: Christian Pease

Figure 18: Felt-tipped pens; 18" × 24"
Title: Self Portrait
Larry, Sonoma State Hospital, California
Age 18. Severely retarded.
Teacher: Connie Butler
Photographer: Christian Pease

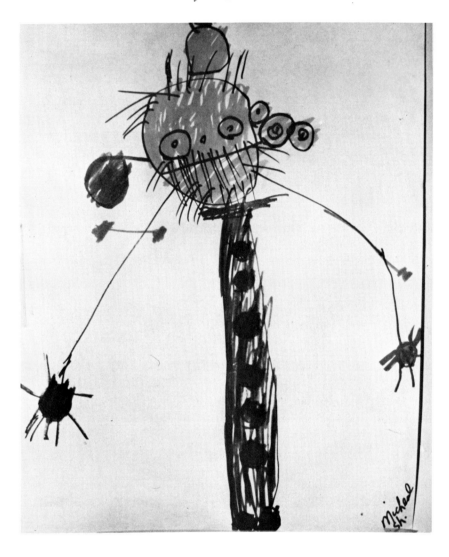

Figure 19: Felt-tipped pens; 18" × 24"
Title: Self Portrait
Michael, Sonoma State Hospital, California
Age 23. Severely retarded.
Teacher: Connie Butler
Photographer: Christian Pease

54486

Figure 20: Tempera; 18" × 24"
Title: Mask
John, Sonoma State Hospital, California
Age 21. Severely retarded.
Teacher: Connie Butler
Photographer: Christian Pease

Figure 21: Crayon: 9" × 12"
Micky, Southbury Training School, Connecticut
Age 38. Moderately retarded, echolalic.
Teacher: Jay Virbutis
Micky does this kind of drawing very quickly. He especially likes to draw the schoolroom and the people in it, paying attention to wall and ceiling details. His drawings show a keen sense of observation and an intuitive feeling for picture space. The crayon is put on thickly with every bit of paper covered with pigment. His color selection is dramatic with a sure use of dark line and mass to contrast with the bright tones.
Photographer: Mack McCormack

Figure 22: Crayon; 9" × 12"
Micky, Southbury Training School, Connecticut
Age 38. Moderately retarded, echolalic.
Teacher: Jay Virbutis
Images from newspapers, advertisements, or whatever catches his eye are combined seemingly at random. The total result, however, is a new composition such as this in which a reclining adult figure is surrounded by a half circle of watching and waiting children.
Photographer: Mack McCormack

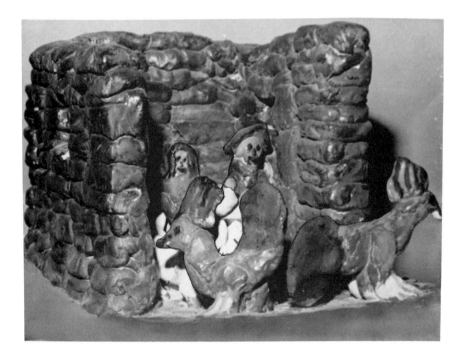

Figure 23: Ceramic, bisque fired and painted with tempera; 8" × 8" × 8"
Title: Nativity Setting
Modesto, Los Lunas Hospital and Training School, New Mexico
Age 45. Severely retarded.
Teacher: Henry Perea
Modesto especially enjoys drawing and painting and this piece was a new experience in a different medium. He "works deliberately and meticulously and wants the different aspects of the work to be near perfection as he sees it. He does indeed work alone and becomes so engrossed in his work that one hardly notices he is there. There is a sort of indifference about him in his daily routine, but art activity seems to provide a rather important outlet for him."
Photographer: Henry Perea

Figure 24: Crayon, 13½" × 11½"
Title: My Friend
Doris, Pennhurst Center, Pennsylvania
Age 25. Severely retarded, Down's syndrome, vision, speech, and hearing impairment.
Teacher: Adelle F. Headley
Photographer: Robert Shoup

Figure 25: Crayon; 12" × 18"
Title: Trish
Doris, Pennhurst Center, Pennsylvania.
Age 25. Severely retarded, Down's syndrome, vision, speech, and hearing impairment.
Teacher: Adelle F. Headley
Photographer: Robert Shoup

Figure 26: Crayon; 18" x 24"
Title: Zoo
Denise, Enid State School, Oklahoma
Age 21. Moderately retarded.
Teacher: M.D.
Denise is a very creative girl who is extremely spontaneous with her work. She was upset the day she drew this. I said "Let's see if you could draw something to make you happy. Where would you like to be?" She said "the zoo." She drew this completely from memory having been to a zoo only once three years earlier. There are, from upper left to the right going down, bats, tiger, snakes, zebra, giraffe, lion, fish, and monkeys in the trees. She came to class upset. By the time she finished her picture an hour and a half later she was happy.
Photographer: J.T. & S.P.

Figure 27: Crayon and felt-tipped pens; 18" × 24"
Title: Spring Flowers
Darrell, Enid State School, Oklahoma
Age 14. Moderately retarded.
Teacher: M.D.
Photographer: J.T. & S.P.

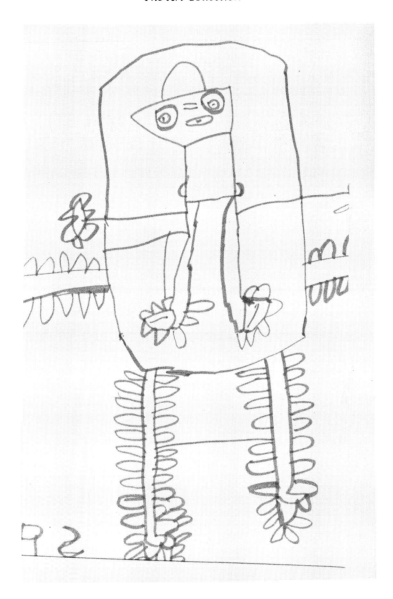

Figure 28: Felt-tipped pen; 15" × 19"
Title: Portrait of Ann
Sharon, Ebensburg Center, Pennsylvania
Age 25. Moderately retarded.
Teacher: Edward J. Klezek
Photographer: Brian Smith

Figures 29 and 30: Crayon; 9" × 12"
Doug, Celentano School, New Haven, Connecticut
Age 18. Down's syndrome.
Teacher: Joan Courcey
"My regular method of teaching art is to integrate it with all aspects of the curriculum," states this teacher. She tries "to make art a vital aspect of each student's program by using art as a reinforcement of other skills," and she believes that "art can be a tool for teaching math, social skills, reading, etc. ." The drawings shown here were done during a lesson "centered around the students recognizing the physical need for getting enough sleep."
Photographer: Joy Sherman

Figure 31: Oil on canvas board; 16" × 20"
Clifford, Southbury Training School, Connecticut
Age 42, Mildly retarded.
Photographer: Joy Sherman

Figure 32: Oil on cardboard; 54" × 28"
Clifford, Southbury Training School, Connecticut
Age 41. Mildly retarded.
Teacher: Russ Huff
One of Clifford's fine paintings done about 1971. The rhythmic quality of
the tree branches in the foreground and the individually stylized foliage
patterns in the background create a harmonious contrast of form and tonal
values. His love for surface pattern is seen in the grass, bark, and bricks. This
painting was done during his last year at the school before going into the
community.
Photographer: Henry Gorski

Figure 33: Oil on canvas board; 16" × 20"
Title: Abstraction
Clifford, Southbury Training School, Connecticut
Age 43. Mildly retarded.
The tightly knit organization of this exceptional painting with its mosaic-like areas and varied surface patterns has the sureness and control which this artist continually exhibits in his work. This particular painting was done while Clifford was living in the community and working at the Goodwill Industries.
Photographer: Henry Gorski

Figure 34: Linoleum blockprint; 4" × 6"
Title: Christmas Angel
Altea, Southbury Training School, Connecticut
Age 21. Mildly retarded.
Teacher: Russ Huff
There is an intensification of the holiday spirit in this dramatically simple design. The organization of the light and dark areas and the choice of images are evidence of the selective eye of the artist. This design was used for the cover of the Holiday Calendar for the Training School in 1961.
Photographer: Joy Sherman

Figure 35: Pencil; 9" × 12"
Title: Head
Eugene, Southbury Training School, Connecticut
Age 14. Moderately retarded.
Teacher: Russ Huff
This striking head owes its monumental effect to the simplification of form and the stripping away of nonessentials. It was done as part of a three-part lesson. Eugene grew in expressive ability and in self-confidence as the teacher carefully provided the climate for creative growth.
Photographer: Joy Sherman

Figure 36: Crayon; 12" × 18"
Mark, Southbury Training School, Connecticut.
Age 14. Profoundly retarded.
Teacher: Russ Huff
An arresting figure in profile which has a curious air of mystery about it.
Photographer: Joy Sherman

Figure 37: Clay; 10" × 12"
Title: Girls' Head
Louise, Southbury Training School, Connecticut
Age 14. Mildly retarded.
Teacher: Russ Huff
A strong forthright piece of sculpture with a hint of pain in the expression.
Photographer: Mack McCormack

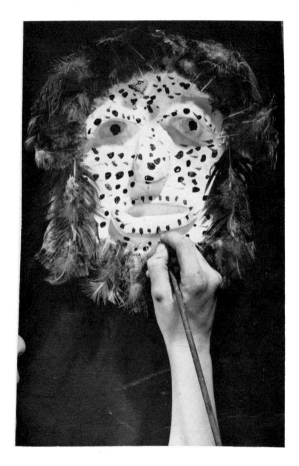

Figure 38: Papier mâché; 18" × 14"
Title: Mask
John, Southbury Training School, Connecticut.
Age 16. Mildly retarded.
Teacher: Russ Huff
This mask was selected for use in Studio One's television production of *A Child Is Waiting.*
Photographer: Mack McCormack

Figure 39: Papier mâché
Southbury Training School, Connecticut
Done by a group of mildly and moderately retarded residents.
Teacher: Russ Huff
The feather and beadwork were all done by one boy who was especially skillful in this kind of detailed ornamentation.
Photographer: Mack McCormack

Figure 40: Poster paint and applied cotton.
Southbury Training School, Connecticut
Done by a group of mildly and moderately retarded residents.
Teacher: Russ Huff
These varied interpretations are refreshingly individual. The Van Gogh-like head in the lower right corner is an example of a different tempo.
Photographer: Mack McCormack

Figure 41: Pencil; 9" × 12"
Title: Self Portrait
Genie, Lives at home in Connecticut
Age 56. Down's syndrome.
One of the many self-portraits Genie does. He is chiefly interested in drawing
people and sometimes works from a newspaper photograph which reminds
him of a friend or a member of the family.
Photographer: Joy Sherman

Figures 42 and 43: Acrylic paint on fabric; Church Vestments.
Andre, Temple School, New Britain, Connecticut
Age 21. Down's syndrome.
Teacher: Don Newcomb
Andre's dramatic painted panels were made into church vestments by Elizabeth Von Dreele and Nona Clague. This activity stemmed from a seminar on The Theology of Social Concern conducted by Dr. Werner Rode at Berkeley Divinity and Yale Divinity School. These two particular vestments were photographed at Andre's exhibition at Quinnipiac College in Hamden, Connecticut and are presently in the collection of the Reverend James Clague.
Photographer: Instructional Resources, Quinnipiac College.

Figure 44: Felt-tipped pens on rice paper; 15" X 16"
Title : Crucifixion
Andre, Temple School, New Britain, Connecticut
Age 21. Down's syndrome.
Teacher: Don Newcomb
This unique and compelling painting is one of the many works by Andre using Christ and stories from the Bible as themes. One cannot look at this stark painting without a stirring of the pulse. The blocked and striped figure has an emotional power which the mere reproduction of natural features seldom achieves.
From *Performance,* 1972. Courtesy of The President's Committee on Employment of the Handicapped, Washington, D.C.

Figure 45: Felt-tipped pens, 20" × 30"
Title: Cain and Abel
Andre, Temple School, New Britain, Connecticut
Age 21. Down's syndrome.
Teacher: Don Newcomb
Another of Andre's magnificent interpretations of a Bible story. There is both expressiveness and formal power in the placement of the two figures in this beautifully composed painting.
Photographer: Henry Gorski

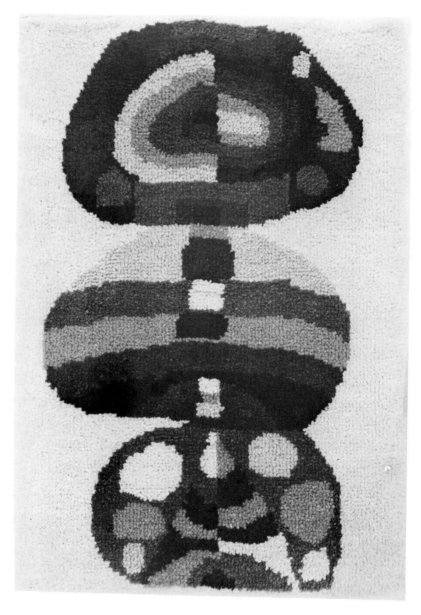

Figure 46: Hooked rug wall hanging; 3' × 4'
Design by Andre, Hooking by Ellen Neilsen.
Teacher: Don Newcomb
Photographer: Henry Gorski

Figure 47: Andre and Don
A happy pupil with his teacher.
Photographer: Rodney Smith

Figure 48: Crayon; 8½" × 11"
Title: Walruses
Charlotte, Alaska
Age 29. Moderately retarded.
Teacher: Fred Schroeter
With what economy of means Charlotte has caught the spirit of the cold north and the quintessential walrusness of these animals!
Photographer: Joy Sherman

Figure 49: Felt-tipped pens, 24" × 20"
Title: Birds in Flight
Scott, Alaska
Age 22. Moderately retarded.
Teacher: Fred Schroeter
This painting is especially effective in color with an orange sun, black birds and tree tops against a pinkish red sky. The composition suggests a sense of infinite space.
Photographer: Fred Schroeter

Figure 50: Felt-tipped pen and cut paper; 24" × 20"
Title: From My Head
Teresa, Alaska
Age 16. Mildly retarded.
Teacher: Fred Schroeter
Photographer: Fred Schroeter

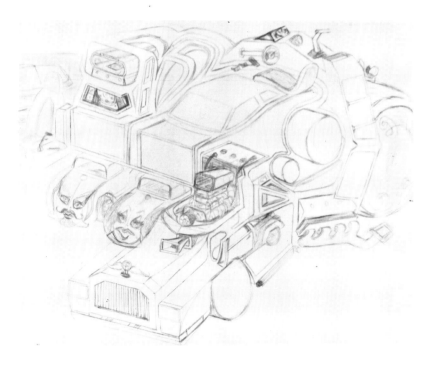

Figure 51: Pencil; 18" × 22"
Joe, Fort Wayne State Hospital and Training Center, Indiana
Age 25. Dull normal, deaf.
Teacher: Eleanore Lyon
"Joe does his drawing for leisure time activities."
Photographer: William Young

Figure 52: Felt-tipped pens and crayon; 18" × 24"
Title: Frankenstein
Denise, Enid State School, Oklahoma
Age 21. Moderately retarded.
Teacher: M.D.
"Denise drew this about a year ago. She likes monsters . . . this is her version
of Frankenstein. His face and hands are green."
Photographer: J.T. & S.P.

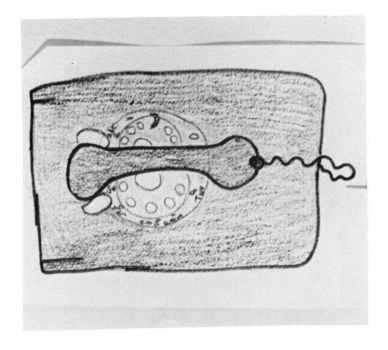

Figure 53: Crayon; 9" × 12"
Title: Telephone
Farris, Enid State School, Oklahoma
Age 27. Moderately retarded.
Teacher: S.M.P.
"Farris decided to do this all on her own. Looking at the telephone she drew what she saw."
Photographer: J.T. & S.P.

Figure 54: Crayon and felt-tipped pens; 9" × 12"
Steve, Enid State School, Oklahoma
Age 20. Moderately retarded.
Teacher: S.M.P.
Photographer: J.T. & S.P.

Figure 55: Yarn and burlap; 25" × 27"
Title: Football Player
Farris, Enid State School, Oklahoma
Age 27. Moderately retarded.
Teacher: V.R.
"Farris drew this directly on red burlap while looking at a statue which stands approximately 10" × 12" high. She gathered her own materials and used her own ideas in color and method."
Photographer: J.T. & S.P.

Figure 56: Shoe box, construction paper, felt-tipped pens; 5½" × 10½"
Robert, Fort Wayne State Hospital and Training Center, Indiana
Age 40. Mildly retarded.
Teacher: Eleanore Lyon
Photographer: William Young

Figure 57: Crayon; 9" × 12"
Title: Shirley
Denise, Enid State School, Oklahoma
Age 21. Moderately retarded.
Teacher: M.D.
This is Denise's version of another instructor. "All the drawings by Denise were done in her spare time after she finished other projects. Many times she has stayed up to two and a half or three hours because she can work on her own."
Photographer: J.T. & S.P.

Figure 58: Crayon and pencil; 18" × 15"
Steve, Enid State School, Oklahoma
Age 20. Moderately retarded.
Teacher: S.M.P.
"This is Steve's own developed style of drawing . . . and was done outside of the Arts and Crafts department. He enjoys art very much . . . and likes to do things his own way."
Photographer: J.T. & S.P.

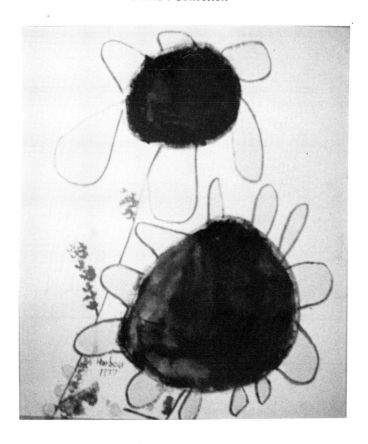

Figure 59: Acrylic paint on canvas; 15" × 17"
Billie, San Angelo Center, Texas
Age 58. Moderately retarded.
Teacher: Jo Lightfoot
Photographer: Doug Hubbart

Figure 60: Crayon; 18" × 24"
Title: Mount Rushmore
Denise, Enid State School, Oklahoma
Age 21. Moderately retarded.
Teacher: M.D.
"Denise had studied about presidents at academic school and they talked about Mount Rushmore . . . and that's what she wanted to draw. The tree and bird she added on her own saying 'There are probably trees there too.'"
This was done about two years ago.
Photographer: J.T. & S.P.

Figure 61: Crayon on sandpaper; 9" × 11"
Title: Me
Andy, Pennhurst Center, Pennsylvania
Age 25. Down's syndrome, impaired speech and vision.
Teacher: Adelle F. Headley
Photographer: Robert Shoup

Figure 62: Colored chalk: 12" × 18"
Title: Me
Jimmie, Pennhurst Center, Pennsylvania
Age 26. Severely retarded.
Teacher: Adelle F. Headley
Photographer: Robert Shoup

Figure 63: Acrylic paint; 17" × 20"
Title: My House
Shirley, Ebensburg Center, Pennsylvania
Age 18. Moderately retarded.
Teacher: Edward J. Klezek
Photographer: Brian Smith

Figure 64: Crayon; 12" × 24"
Title: Waiting
Denise, Enid State School, Oklahoma
Age 21. Moderately retarded.
Teacher: M.D.
"She liked birds and said she wanted to draw a mother bird. In this picture the mother bird is waiting for the eggs to hatch so she can feed the babies a worm."
Photographer: J.T. & S.P.

Figure 65: Clay; 3" high
Title: Kitty Cat
Doris, Pennhurst Center, Pennsylvania
Age 25. Severely retarded, Down's syndrome, vision, speech, and hearing impairment.
Teacher: Adelle F. Headley
Photographer: Robert Shoup

Figure 66: Crayon; 12" × 18"
Title: My Friend
Violet, Pennhurst Center, Pennsylvania
Age 49. Mildly retarded, speech and vision impairment.
Teacher: Adelle F. Headley
Photographer: Robert Shoup

Figures 67 and 68: Ceramic
Bob, Syracuse Developmental Center, New York
Age 23. Severely retarded.
Teacher: Christine Drozd
Photographer: David Blatchley

Figure 69: Ceramic
John, Syracuse Developmental Center, New York
Age 24. Severely retarded.
Teacher: Christine Drozd
Photographer: David Blatchley

Figure 70: Mixed media on canvas; 36" × 24"
Title: Thanksgiving Time
Sam, Southbury Training School, Connecticut
Age 39. Mildly retarded.
This painting, like all others, was done on Sam's own time after he had finished his duties at the school store. In good weather he can be found at an outdoor table in the picnic grove near the lake which is a pleasant recreation spot on the grounds.
Photographer: Henry Gorski

Figure 71: Oil on the back of vinyl; 36" × 24"
Title: Fall Time
Sam, Southbury Training School, Connecticut
Age 39. Mildly retarded.
Photographer: Henry Gorski

Figure 72: Mixed media on canvas board, 24" × 30"
Title: Covered Bridge By The Water
Sam, Southbury Training School, Connecticut
Age 39. Mildly retarded.
Photographer: Henry Gorski

Figure 73: Oil wash and burning tool on pressed board; 8" × 16"
Title: Indian Weaving
Sam, Southbury Training School, Connecticut
Age 39. Mildly retarded.
Photographer: Henry Gorski

Figure 74: Mixed media on burlap; 20" × 50"
Title: Sun Parlor
Sam, Southbury Training School, Connecticut
Age 39. Mildly retarded.
Sam brought this up from the basement storeroom in his cottage to show us. There is no room in the cottage quite like this. "I make them up" he said in reference to this and all his other paintings.
Photographer: Henry Gorski

Figure 75: Crayon; 24" × 27"
Title: Dog
William, Ebensburg Center, Pennsylvania
Age 22. Severely retarded.
Teacher: Edward Klezek
Photographer: Brian Smith

Figure 76: Tempera resist; 12" × 15"
Title: Fire
Kenneth, Ebensburg Center, Pennsylvania
Age 23. Severely retarded.
Teacher. Edward Klezek
Photographer: Brian Smith

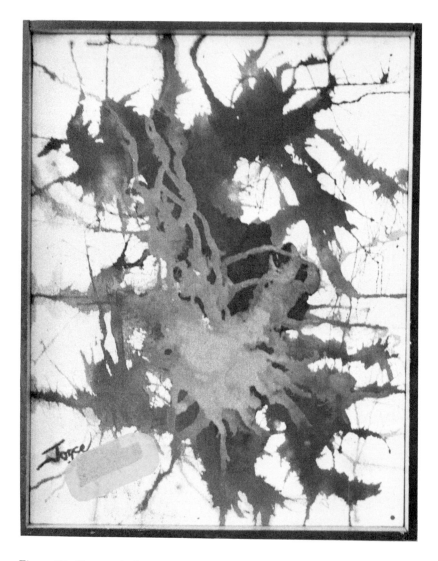

Figure 77: Straw painting, water base paint on stretched fabric; 18" × 24"
Title: Cobweb
Joyce, Ebensburg Center, Pennsylvania
Age 25. Severely retarded.
Teacher: Edward Klezek
Photographer: Brian Smith

Figure 78: Crayon; 9" × 12"
Title: Cars
Ernest, Southbury Training School, Connecticut
Age 34. Moderately retarded.
Ernest draws trucks and cars almost exclusively, always using direct line and
his own special way of designing.
Photographer: Joy Sherman

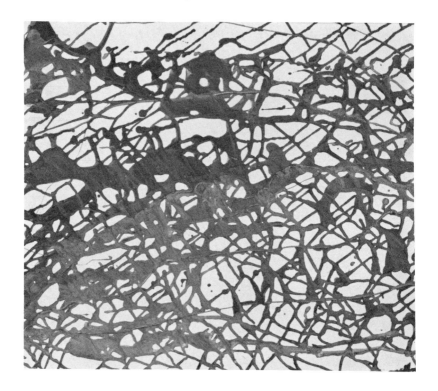

Figure 79: Tempera; 22" × 25"
Title: Webs
Earl, Ebensburg Center, Pennsylvania
Age 38. Severely retarded.
Teacher: Edward J. Klezek
Photographer: Brian Smith

Figure 80: Clay; 5½" and 2½"
This charming pair of rabbits was bought some years ago at the Southbury Training School fair. No one has been able to identify the maker so they shall ever remain anonymous.
Photographer: Mack McCormack

Figure 81: Felt-tipped pens; 20" x 27"
Title: Adam and Eve
Andre, Temple School, New Britain, Connecticut
Age 22. Down's syndrome.
Teacher: Don Newcomb
Another original interpretation of a Biblical theme. The severely formal design and the simple directness of the line technique give this age-old theme a compelling power.
Photographer: Richard Grave

Figure 82: Pencil. 9" × 12"
Genie, Lives at home in Connecticut
Age 56. Down's syndrome.
Genie is very friendly and out-going and likes to draw people. He has lived all his life as a member of a large household.
Photographer: Joy Sherman

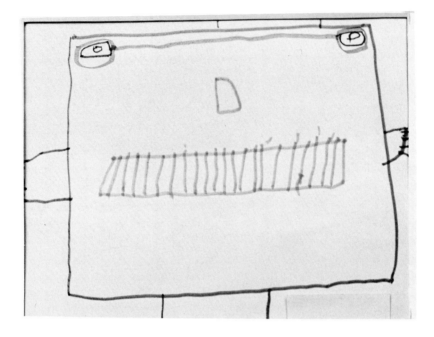

Figure 83: Felt-tipped pens; 10" × 13"
Title: The Man
Iggy, Southington Association for Retarded Citizens, Connecticut
Age 60. Severely retarded.
Teacher: Rose Kukhala
An imaginative rendition of a head whose disciplined use of space adds an intensity of expressions.
Photographer: Henry Gorski

Figure 84: Felt-tipped pens; 14" × 20"
Ernie, Convalescent Home, Connecticut
Age 65. Severely handicapped.
Teacher: Justine Gonyea
A marvelously detailed country scene in which houses, horses, and grass are skillfully woven together in a rich pattern.
Photographer: Henry Gorski

Figure 85: Watercolor; 12" × 18"
Title: Cowboy
Joan, Enid State School, Oklahoma
Age 26. Moderately retarded.
Teacher: S.M.P.
"This was done two years ago at which time Joan was very creative and loved art. She drew and painted with bright colors and came up with some amazing things."
Photographer: J.T. & S.P.

Figure 86: Acrylic paint on canvas; 20" × 30"
Title: Circus
David, Muskegon Developmental Center, Michigan
Age 16. Down's syndrome.
Teacher: G.M.B.
Photographer: Jeff Gutsell

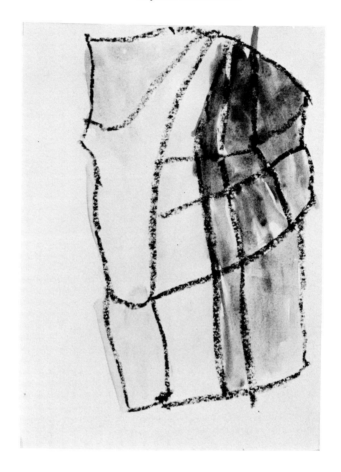

Figure 87: Watercolor and crayon; 8" × 10"
Lee, Muskegon Developmental Center, Michigan
Age 13. Moderately retarded.
Teacher: G.M.B.
Photographer: Jeff Gutsell

Figures 88, 89, 90, and 91: Crayon. 9" × 12"
In 1965 these drawings from the Southbury Training School were printed as postcards and sold for the benefit of the school. Each one of the figures is a bold original statement sparkling with its own individual style.
Photographer: Joy Sherman

Figure 92: Felt-tipped pen; 18" × 24"
Title: Tiger
Karl, Sonoma State Hospital, California
Age 18. Severely retarded.
Teacher: Connie Butler
Photographer: Christian Pease

Figure 93: Felt-tipped pens; 18" × 24"
Title: Face Gallery
Michael, Sonoma State Hospital, California
Age 23. Severely retarded.
Teacher: Connie Butler
Photographer: Christian Pease

Figures 94 and 95: 9" × 12"
Micky, Southbury Training School, Connecticut
Age 38. Moderately retarded, echolalic.
Teacher: Jay Virbutis
The classroom holds endless fascination for Micky and he delights in showing details of interior architecture which he handles with an intuitive sense of perspective.
Photographer: Mack McCormack

Figure 96: Felt-tipped pen; 5" × 24"
Title: Halloween
Edward, Enid State School, Oklahoma
Age 54. Moderately retarded.
Teacher: D.O.
"Edward has his own style . . . He usually draws huge murals which he loves to do. Holidays are his favorites. He can tell you all about them and what he is drawing."
Photographer: J.T. & S.P.

Figure 97: Felt-tipped pen; 12½" × 31"
Title: Crucifixion
Mark, Temple School, New Britain, Connecticut
Age 19. Down's syndrome.
Teacher: Don Newcomb
This astonishing painting has the brilliance of stained glass.
Photographer: Henry Gorski

Figure 98: Poster paint; 22" × 28"
Title: Happy
Edward, New Horizons Adult Program, Connecticut
Age 25. Down's syndrome.
Photographer: Henry Gorski

Figure 99: Felt-tipped pen; 10" × 13"
Title. Without a Name
Frank, Southington Association for Retarded Citizens, Connecticut.
Age 70.
Teacher: Rose Kukhala
Photographer: Henry Gorski

Figure 100: Felt-tipped pen; 18" × 16"
Laura, Temple School, New Britain, Connecticut
Age 17. Down's syndrome.
Teacher: Don Newcomb
Photographer: Henry Gorski

Figure 101: Felt-tipped pen; 18" × 16"
Laura, Temple School, New Britain, Connecticut
Age 17. Down's syndrome.
Teacher: Don Newcomb
We can smile in appreciation of the imagination which created this fanciful
animal composition.
Photographer: Henry Gorski

Figure 102: Plywood construction with plastic and leather; 16" × 42"
Title: Guitar
Zigfredo, Chamberlin School, New Britain, Connecticut
Age 19. Brain damaged.
Teacher: Don Newcomb
Zigfredo loves to construct airplanes and other objects from wood. He is particularly adept at embellishment details such as the plastic circles at the top and the leather strap ornamentations.
Photographer: William Boyle

Figure 103: Felt-tipped pen and acrylic paint on rice paper; 8" × 12"
Title: Moon Child
Larry, Temple School, New Britain, Connecticut
Age 14. Mildly retarded.
Teacher: Don Newcomb
Photographer: Henry Gorski

Figure 104: Watercolors; 9" × 12"
Title: Cityscape
Andre, Temple School, New Britain, Connecticut
Age 19. Down's syndrome.
Teacher: Don Newcomb
This painting was done in conjunction with a unit of study on "Where We
Live: Connecticut Towns and Cities."
Photography: Henry Gorski

Figure 105: Watercolors; 9" × 12"
Title: Cat
Mark, Temple School, New Britain, Connecticut
Age 19, Down's syndrome.
Teacher: Don Newcomb
A wonderfully ferocious striped feline.
Photographer: Henry Gorski

Figure 106: Felt-tipped pens; 9" × 12"
Title: Brothers
Mark, Temple School, New Britain, Connecticut
Age 19. Down's syndrome.
Teacher: Don Newcomb
Photographer: Henry Gorski

Figure 107: Felt-tipped pens; 9" × 12"
Title: Portrait of the Teacher
David, Temple School, New Britain, Connecticut
Age 19. Mildly retarded.
Teacher: Don Newcomb
Photographer: Henry Gorski

Figure 108: Crayon; 6" × 9"
Betty, Temple School, New Britain, Connecticut
Age 18. Mildly retarded.
Teacher: Don Newcomb
Photographer: Henry Gorski

Figure 109: Felt-tipped pens; 12" x 18"
Title: Birthdays
Laura, Temple School, New Britain, Connecticut
Age 17. Down's syndrome.
Teacher: Don Newcomb
Each month the class celebrated the birthdays of all those who were born in that month. This painting is Laura's interpretation of a triple birthday party.
Photographer: Henry Gorski

Figure 110: Felt-tipped pens; 13" × 15"
Mark, Temple School, New Britain, Connecticut
Age 19. Down's syndrome.
Teacher: Don Newcomb
Photographer: Henry Gorski

Figure 111: Felt-tipped pens; 13" × 18"
Title: Crucifixion
Mark, Temple School, New Britain, Connecticut
Age 19. Down's syndrome.
Teacher: Don Newcomb
Photographer: Henry Gorski

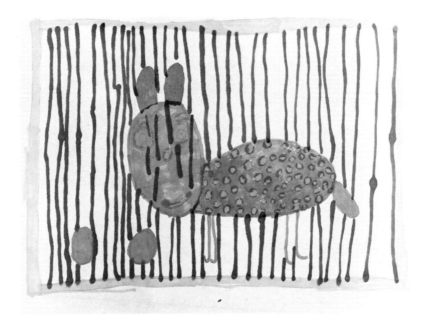

Figure 112: Felt-tipped pens; 12" × 18"
Title: Caged Animal
Laura, Temple School, New Britain, Connecticut
Age 17. Down's syndrome.
Teacher: Don Newcomb
A painting done after a trip to the Bronx Zoo.
Photographer: Henry Gorski

Figure 113: Felt-tipped pens; 12" × 18"
Title: Man
Andre, Temple School, New Britain, Connecticut
Age 19. Down's syndrome.
Teacher: Don Newcomb
This is an example from Andre's *Man* series. It is done in brilliant primary
colors.
Photographer: Henry Gorski

Figure 114: Cloth collage, paint and glue; 15" × 20"
Title: Self Portrait
Anne, Temple School, New Britain, Connecticut
Age 19. Down's syndrome.
Teacher: Don Newcomb
Photographer: Henry Gorski

Figure 115: Textile paint on linen; 15" × 20"
Larry, Temple School, New Britain, Connecticut
Age 15. Mildly retarded.
Teacher: Don Newcomb
One marvels at the skillful use of tonal pattern in this arresting painting.
Photographer: Henry Gorski

Figure 116: Crayon; 12" × 18"
James, Enid State School, Oklahoma
Age 35. Severely retarded.
Teacher: S.M.D.
"James loves to draw and participates in Art and Crafts. He always draws interesting things and concentrates very hard on his work. I cannot always understand him when he explains what he had drawn."
Photographer: J.T. & S.P.

Figure 117: Crayon; 12" × 18"
Darlene, Celentano School, New Haven, Connecticut
Age 10. Moderately retarded.
Teacher. Patricia Cawley
Photographer: Joy Sherman

Figure 118: Yarn and wood; 23½ × 8"
Bill, Fort Wayne Hospital and Training Center, Indiana
Age 25. Mildly retarded.
Teacher: Eleanore Lyon
Photographer: William Young

Figure 119: Yarn, mosaic stone, and plywood; 16" × 20"
William, Ebensburg Center, Pennsylvania
Age 22. Severely retarded.
Teacher: Edward J. Klezek
Photographer: Brian Smith

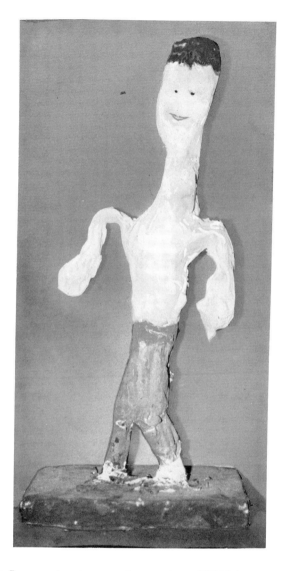

Figure 120: Paper and paste over wire armature; 20" high
Title: Man
John, Los Lunas Hospital and Training School, New Mexico
Age 18. Severely retarded.
Teacher: Henry Perea
Photographer: Henry Perea

Figure 121. Crayon on old pillow case; 20" x 30"
John, Southbury Training School, Connecticut
Age 30. Moderately retarded.
John draws whenever he can get a piece of cloth to work on. This is an example of the unusually designed heads he does.
Photographer: Joy Sherman

Figure 122: Pencil; 11" × 17"
Title: Wagon Train
Doris, Pennhurst Center, Pennsylvania
Age 25. Severely retarded, Down's syndrome, vision, speech, and hearing impairment.
Teacher: Adelle F. Headley
Photographer: Robert Shoup

Chapter III _____

SOME TEACHERS AND
THEIR EXPERIENCES

THE teachers are those who work directly with the handicapped and it is enlightening to read what they have to say about their methods and experiences. Several spoke of the sometimes discouraging lack of a kindred spirit with whom to talk things over. The pleasures and insights gained from certain special situations are deepened and sometimes clarified by a sharing of them with others involved in similar work.

Connie Butler of Sonoma, California teaches an art program in a unit for severely retarded young adults, many of whom have additional medical problems. The program has been very successful despite this. "The walls of the unit are covered with paintings and we have an enthusiastic group of admirers but not a very wide public."

Like many other teachers working with the handicapped she stressed the value of creative art experiences as a vital ingredient in their lives:

Creative activity is important for everyone and almost everyone wants to create if given half a chance. I believe this is a basic human need, right under food and shelter. With simple materials the retarded can express themselves freely. The results are amazingly beautiful, abstract, unself-conscious, and spontaneous. Many have a natural talent for balance, form, and color relationships.

Art adds to a sense of identity. Each resident has his own style and when the art is hung up around the unit it not only brightens the place but is a source of pride to the artists. Seeing their work hung gives the residents a sense of accomplishment. They enjoy the activity of working. It's fun, relaxing, personal, and reassuring.

In an institution where there is usually a lack of individual expression this is particularly important.

Since those in residential programs have only the immediate staff as a pseudo-family "The individual's need for love, recognition, and identity" become the responsibility of the staff. Creative projects help the residents gain "a sense of accomplishment and pride."

There are no specific goals in my art program. People progress at their own rate. Usually there is very little progression from one stage to another, just an amplification in using various media as the residents become more assured in what they are doing.

I use simple materials as in pre-school work: tempera paint, large 18" x 24" paper, finger paints, crayons, felt-tipped pens, large scissors, printing with styrofoam blocks, brayers, water base inks, clay, and colored chalk for a large blackboard.

Christine Drozd, an art student at Syracuse University, worked at the Syracuse Developmental Center through the Community Internship Program. From May to August she spent approximately fifteen hours a week helping with lunch, playing some form of basketball or catch with residents, and also visiting casually with them. All were severely or profoundly retarded adults between twenty and forty years old. They showed "an incredible difference in abilities and interests."

After getting to know the residents and my fellow workers on the unit, we came up with the idea of taking the men to the University for lunch and to work in a classroom. The emphasis was on getting the men outside and in a routine once a week. We either took bag lunches or ate at a place on campus, spending a lot of time familiarizing the men with the variety to be found on a large university campus. The three men who went together one day a week were all able to get around by themselves, but would not be able to take a bus by themselves. Busing there was an important part of the day. The men were usually picked up from the campus by someone from our unit so we could spend more time working in the classroom. The room we used was large and almost all windows. They enjoyed the view. Several sturdy desks were pushed together to form one big table and everyone sat around on a chair or stool. We had a chalkboard and plenty of stoneware clay which I had mixed up. We used simple hand building methods, pinching, rolling, throwing out slabs, and a little coiling. As an art student familiar with the clay medium myself, I was surprised at how easily each man "took" to the clay. There was very little hesitation over what to make, and the way each man worked was definitely an individual expressive act. One of the men was legally blind and did many thinly pinched bowls, always working in a very intense manner. Another would make little "families" of pinched, fat bottomed figures in varying sizes. Two of the men would often copy each other on a new method. I did the firing and glazing of all the pieces since my scheduled time did not allow for the men to be with me when I was able to fire. A very simple ash glaze was used, just to finish things off, but not as decoration. If I did this another time, I would have them glaze their own pieces. I spent time helping each with his own work, and we did a few larger pieces all together, slab formed around other shapes such as bottles.

This teacher emphasized that making objects in clay was only one part of the whole experience. Traveling by bus, eating lunch, going to the classroom, and walking to various spots on the campus were of equal value to the young adults involved in this program.

Concerning the art created under her supervision, she feels that it is an important means of self-expression and somewhat therapeutic as well. "The process of working with clay can provide quite an emotional release. It does for me and I think it definitely did for my men from the Center."

The value of such programs is not only for the handicapped. This young teacher goes on to say that "This was the most meaniful learning experience I had all through my school career."

Henry Perea of New Mexico has been a teacher of the handicapped for twenty years. At Los Lunas Hospital and Training School he works with the full range of disabilities from educable to profoundly retarded, including the multi-handicapped. Art materials are used to stimulate sight, thought, and movement, always starting from where the particular pupil *is* at the time. "The same art materials that can be used with some cognizance and organization by higher level students can be used in a non-objective stimulating manner with lower levels."

He suggests this approach for those handicapped who are hard to reach: "Any resource beginning with your own gentleness and patience, to giving the child a chance to hold, to touch, to move, or to smell, is valid." He too is convinced of the importance of art in education: I can sincerely say that no field is more grossly neglected in our country's school curriculms than is art; yet without thinking and quite unconsciously, most teachers utilize art as the most concrete method of putting their particular subject matter across to their pupils. Why? Because art is an inborn thing. All first experiences of the child are sensory in nature and hence, intimately related to the very natural reactions and responses that very basic art experiences entail. In other words, if a child can participate through art experiences his sensory experiences, he is taking part in some form of expression.

These teachers have discovered and refined methods which work for them in their individual situations. They are convinced of the real value of using creative art experiences in training the handicapped, and their attitude is perhaps best summed up in this statement by a teacher at Ebensburg Center, Pennsylvania. "It is my opinion," says Edward J. Klezek, "that there is a much undeveloped potential within each retardate."

He has developed a method of teaching wherein he often demonstrates the activity and then encourages the pupil to try to do it independently. Sometimes "physical and verbal promptings" are given or "manual guidance is necessary." He uses "continuous positive reinforcement . . . expressed in social praise." In describing his method further, he stressed the complete freedom given to express individuality. Even though the attention span for most pupils is short, he uses a variety of materials to stimulate the senses: "bright colors for visual stimulation; clay, finger paints, sand, and mosaics for tactile stimulation."

The experience itself is the important thing, he concluded: "I feel that the learning experience is more important than the finished product."

Methods are made to be adapted to individual circumstances. They alone will not solve educational problems, nor guarantee that the pupil will grow. The imagination and personality of the teacher are of the greatest importance in giving life and meaning to the best designed plans. G.M.B., a teacher at the Muskegon Developmental Center in Michigan had this to say: "I believe that one must like the retarded, like their personalities, and believe in them as human beings capable of giving and receiving love . . . and one must like art, art for enjoyment . . . and take a deep breath, say 'hello,' smile, and begin."

She usually holds classes in a large art room, but sometimes uses the dormitories where the residents live. Warm weather may find them working outside. "I use tactile stimulation materials, collage materials, clay, paint, and music. We have a variety of *junk* which has been donated and which I keep in a box. The people love putting their hand in the box." This box full of surprises not only adds to the interest of the class, but also to the variety of creative possibilities and experiences. B.M.B. states further that — There is the therapeutic value of art in stimulating the mental and motor coordination of the developmentally disabled. Eye-hand coordination, shape recognition, fine and gross motor coordination, sublimation, perception, etc. etc. are all developed by the use of art in teaching the retarded.

They need art and usually love it. They need the stimulation and the freedom to explore their environment and their abilities with *no failure* attached.

. . . and there is another school of thought, that of the development of the brain: that the left hemisphere is the seat of analysis and sequential thinking and learning, while the right is superior in visual-spatial abilities. If this is correct, that art comes from the right side of the brain, then it is critically important that we work with the developmentally disabled in art.

But besides all of the above, art *does* stimulate greater body awareness and lessens inhibitions. It is failure free, and above all fun.

Don Newcomb, an unusually sensitive and gifted teacher, works with the retarded in New Britain, Connecticut. There is an atmosphere of encouragement and acceptance in his class which provides a climate for creative growth. Both the openness of programs and the free atmosphere at the Temple School where he teaches, allows the children to explore and experiment in various educational forms and to find their own potential. This philosophy of beginning with the individual interests of the children, rather than imposing a more traditional program geared to academic achievement, allows children like Andre to develop their talent.

Creative ability varies among the retarded just as it does among those who are not retarded, and this ability is usually outside the scope of aptitude and intelligence. Newcomb and other enlightened professionals believe that any and all art and mechanical skills should be fostered, despite preestablished norms of classification. Newcomb states: The exceptional child is sensitive, often a necessary victim of emotional upsets and trauma. Andre and his classmates seek loving and the thrill of accomplishment like any other human being. The most ordinary daily success can become a major event. Andre finds this joy in his art. To us, the expressive character of his work reflects a longing for acceptance imposed by physical and mental barriers.

All of Andre's paintings exude a direct simplicity, a sureness of vision and intuitive color sense and form that can well be admired. While these paintings are in the tradition of what is called *l' art brut*, the obvious appeal lies in their apparent artlessness and innocent, almost primitive, observation.

In speaking about his working with Andre, Newcomb says: . . . As his teacher, it did not take long to notice something in his crayon drawings that set him apart from the doodlings and simple forms of most of the other children. In the beginning Andre appeared non-verbal. But surprisingly enough as his drawings matured and became more sophisticated, so did his speech patterns. Even when it was difficult for others to understand him, I felt he spoke through his paintings; this was his mode of communication. . . . his paintings are in fact his only way of talking. All the pain and joy of his response to the world he expresses through his art which gives it tremendous emotional urgency.

After introducing him to new materials, watercolors, oils, rice papers, etc., he improved so much that he was given a small exhibit of felt-tipped marker paintings at the Berkeley Divinity School in New Haven.

Andre listened to Bible stories which Newcomb told him and then proceeded to respond to the ideas and feelings by working with sure fingers and little hesitation. One time he sat before a canvas for almost two hours before starting to paint. "He was thinking all the time, had it all figured out in his head and then went at it."

My classroom was part of a seminar on the "Theology of Social Concern" conducted by Dr. Werner Rode. Because Berkeley was preparing its students for the Episcopal ministry it was not surprising that they would ask Andre to paint within religious motifs. To many students and teachers the intensity and power of his paintings became a form of expressionistic art that would lend itself non-literal interpretations of Biblical stories. This was a time when congregations were making their own vestments in response to a search for new liturgical forms.

"Andre's progress during the past two years has been especially exciting for me," said his teacher at the time of the then seventeen-year-old's exhibition at Columbia University in 1970. "To watch what is now his own inimitable art style emerge from a collection of non-drawings and crayon sketches to the sophisticated renditions of Old and New Testament themes, and the crafting of liturgical vestments, has been rewarding." The paintings and vestments have been widely exhibited and have evoked enthusiastic response wherever they have been seen. There are Andre vestments in cathedrals in Newark and Boston and Japan, and many paintings are in private collections. One of the paintings won the grand prize in an international art competition sponsored by the British National Society for Handicapped Children in London in 1971.

. . . Although Andre does seem to have limited ability to express himself verbally, it does not necessarily mean that his paintings are not meaningful to him, and in a special way, to those who admire his work.

Children's art expressions vary according to their experiences, perceptions, and maturity, and therefore like any genuine artist Andre can, at times, be incredibly superior to other young people with natural talent.

When Andre is drawing he is telling us a story; this is his way of communication, expressing to us in images what in his stories stand for concepts.

In turn his paintings stand by themselves; they can be evaluated and judged on their own merit.

Andre's success, the attention and praise his exhibits have brought him, his joy in his work "engendered what one might surprisingly call a *school* within a school; his own peers want to emulate him and feel encouraged to become as successful as he." This following of fellow students helped him to develop a sense of leadership and accomplishment which increased his poise and contributed to the diminishing of less desirable mannerisms. Another gratifying result was that those who tried to copy his inimitable style "have emerged with original ideas of their own."

"The story of Andre," Newcomb maintains, "is only one example of a handicapped child overcoming the inherent stigma of retardation. He beautifully illustrates that our society, within the context of special programs, can lift the retarded child out of myth-shrouded hopelessness and into the world of self-supporting membership."

Eleanore Lyon, a teacher at the Fort Wayne State Hospital and Training Center, Indiana, speaks of "learning through discovery," and of "using music as a track to teach self-awareness and awareness of environment." She also believes that art is important in the training of the retarded because "it is the best vehicle of therapeutic teaching to assist the retarded to explore his environment and to discover his potential." In addition, she stresses the use of art as a means to "experience success and to develop self-esteem," as well as a means for "constructive use of leisure time."

"One of the most important approaches one can take with the retarded is to be receptive and accepting of all attempts at art," says Jean Courcey of the Celentano School in New Haven. It is also important to provide "meaningful projects," and "to give concrete examples and instructions."

"I feel art provides the retarded with another means of self-expression which is of special benefit to those who are limited in expressing themselves verbally."

She believes in the value of art as a "non-threatening learning experience," especially "if the teacher is responsive and not critical of their work."

Russ Huff, a responsive artist and teacher who more than a decade ago taught at the Southbury Training School for ten years, has contributed some thoughts and conclusions from his experiences. He noticed that within the group labeled retarded there are those who are artistically gifted. Their works showed creative ability in the use of form and color, in power of expression, and in unity of design, equal to the art of the talented normal person. He found that Down's Syndrome individuals often showed a real ability to create plastically unified paintings.

"Too often," he continued, "we have treated the child's products . . . as inferior attempts to reproduce nature. Even if the child showed talent he was usually put in the position of copying, tracing, or coloring in." The assumption was that he could not be 'a real artist' . . . and the "so-called important work for bulletin boards, posters, and program covers," was given to those whose work closely resembled the usual uninspired products which pass for art.

Like many other good teachers he felt that this was wrong, and "only shows our own lack of sensitivity to art forms and expressions, to say nothing of the second rate roll the child is put in."

Since the fulfillment of any child's potential is of the utmost importance, then it is of equal importance that the gifted retarded child be given special experiences to help him reach that fulfillment . . . I think of Clifford, Jay, John, William, Linda and Patty, all artistically gifted, and see the tragedy if we neglect to develop the one area in which nature has made them our superior.

. . . Freedom in art is one way we can find out more about them and reach them as well as their being able to communicate with us. To give them a feeling of a place in our world, but above all, a richness and meaning to their lives, we should leave no stone unturned.

I can contribute in two ways. As an artist I have the ability to recognize and to analyze creative work from an artistic standpoint, and as a teacher I have been able to get them to work in their own individual way.

There was a series of art activities at the Training School which included the Art Club for older residents which met once a week for recreation and leisure time activities, the school Arts and Crafts program for younger trainable and educable groups, and the I.T. Arts and Crafts group for trainable older girls. The main goal of these groups was the development of personality and the learning of minor skills, or as in the O.T. Shop, the art was first and primarily a means of communication between students and therapist.

In 1958 Huff initiated a summer art project. This was the first time he had a block of time in which artistically talented residents were allowed to pursue their creative work. They met for three hours every morning for an eight week period. He selected seventeen boys and girls whom he knew from past experience to be artistically gifted and who had the interest span to work a full morning. Aside from this, there was no age limit or IQ requirement. The goals for the program were "personal expression and aesthetic satisfaction . . . with all other things being by-products."

The program was a great success from the beginning. There were no discipline problems and the students worked hard. "I envied their concentration and devotion to their work . . . I have never seen more interest and intensity of concentration in any professional art school." The feeling of being an individual was very important to them. They had "importance in the art class," and were free to express their views. "They were not just one of a cottage group, or just a name on the books."

Huff observed that each individual wants to retain his identity and "in the artistically gifted there seemed to be an even stronger urge for the creative solitude of the mind which he recognized as being "different from mental withdrawal."

Sandy was one of the participants in this program. One of the best students with an intense interest in his clay work, he was "contentment personified" in this summer session. This, even though the teacher had been warned that he could be violent and had run away after being transferred from another facility.

Hyperactive, impulsive Bill enjoyed being out of his cottage for a time each day doing what he loved to do in art. For the first time the teacher was able to work individually with him and show him some technical pointers, something which could not have been done a year previously.

There were others. Of special interest was a very disturbed boy who would scarcely talk when he first started in this program. His work went from very complex to very simple and as the work grew simpler he began to speak with greater clarity. Another teacher from a different school mentioned how a girl, who was often a behavior problem in the cottage setup, exhibited none of this disruptive behavior in the art class.

One cannot draw final conclusions from incidents like this but it does serve to point out one real value of creative art experiences for the mentally retarded.

There was Clifford, "one of the most talented persons I have ever worked with, including normal children and adults." He had great skill in drawing and painting, seemed to be able to adapt himself to any medium, and worked with astonishing dedication.

He was a good looking young man of twenty-three at that time, very intense in his manner, reminding "me of a self-portrait of Van Gogh." He worked as a house boy and helper in one of the cottages for the severely retarded and was excellent at his work:

The first time he came to my attention was when he brought me a sketch book filled with strange drawings. There were snakes, monsters, devils, and various weapons such as daggers and swords. While they were bizarre, they were also highly creative. Clifford has a tremendous sense of design and composition in his work. Everything he did was a complete statement.

As the years went by he became my star student. The only thing that I could do for Clifford was to provide him with materials to work with. He was never without an idea for a painting.

The only thing I ever asked of Clifford was that he would listen to *no one* as far as criticism or advise concerning his art work.

He is the only real, natural artist that I have met.

A deaf girl was among the other residents Huff worked with. She had regressed in her academic work and had become withdrawn in her cottage but she did very well in this summer program. Art was something she could do. It was a way for her to be noticed, as well as an outlet for her emotions.

Another girl did very interesting work from a psychological point of view, using symbols and an outpouring of ideas on two large six by four foot papers. One boy was amazingly prolific and did about eighty paintings, drawings, and crayon works during the summer. He kept up a continual flow of ideas and impressions of his surrounding, the cottage, the school, the playground, and the bus.

Still another boy, whose history was a series of behavior problems, loved to draw from nature and thoroughly enjoyed painting. The knots of his behavior problems seemed to become untangled when he was in rapport with his canvas. Professional artists who saw this boy's work were impressed with its expressive content and plastic qualities.

Huff is convinced of the importance of this kind of program. "The products and by-products were beautiful and gratifying ... I found that the art was much more interesting when there was more freedom."

The following is a description of an art project done during the regular school year, the making of a clay head using a pancake-like basic form which the children had rolled and shaped themselves.

1. We touched our eyes, emphasizing place on the head and how many (two). Then we used our sticks (the ends) and made two holes for the eyes in the pancake head.
2. We touched our nose, emphasizing placement and number (one) also the fact that it stuck out. Then we added a piece of clay for the nose.
3. The mouth was added after a similar procedure.

The next project was to make a step-by-step drawing of a head. "We added hair and ears, letting the children feel that they had discovered things I had missed."

This project helped them become aware of the parts and the wholeness of the head. This is not copying, for the children actually experienced the things by feeling and creating.

In one class children who had never drawn a head came out with a relatively clear concept of one.

Here is a description of another one of his projects:

All the children wanted to do a clay turkey. I did not want to use a pattern or have them copy, so I worked out a plan. First they were to do their own version with no help from me. Second, I was going to show them a realistic turkey and discuss it with them . . . then do another turkey. Last, I was going to help them, step by step, to make a turkey.

There was just one thing wrong. The children became so interested in doing their own version that I had them work all period and only gave minor suggestions.

When the class finished they had all created some beautiful little clay objects, each one unique. I have never had a class do this so successfully. They also made paintings and crayon drawings of turkeys.

Huff remembered that he had to be careful in doing demonstrations because the children tended to copy, despite being told that they were to use their own ideas. In general he noticed that, "The work of the trainable child seems to indicate more nearly the personality of the child than the work of the educable. The educable child is more easily influenced by outside forces."

Comments and contributions by other teachers have been included in the legends accompanying the pictures. There are many other good teachers working with the developmentally disabled.

The sampling included in this book may indeed be, like the art, the mere tip of an iceberg.

AFTERWORD

DURING the great ice age in Asia parts of China were spared preserving a multitude of flowers. So the destroying glaciers spared some part of these artists enabling them to draw, paint or model these works which move us so, and make us wonder what fossil hopes and possibilities still lie dormant.

One barrier in responding to this art is too quickly putting aside one's sorrow. In trying not to be over sympathetic, one gropes for formuli and reaches for objectivity – civilizing forces often prevent us from responding in a simple, human way. And we are the poorer for it.

One is constantly reminded of primitive art when turning the pages of *Beyond Limitations* – that is primitive art before the divinities fled the carvings of animals, masks and utile things. One remembers its purposeful period when it was sacred and magic, when its creating was done from necessity, its shaping called for and directed by those great secret ceremonies which linked us to an earlier world we all once shared.

The parallels are obvious and many. The vitality, the economy of line echo the purest in archaic forms in wood or bone or cave.

Marguerite Lupap